We know we have a winner here, even if we can't pronounce its name, 'Selbstfahrlafette (Sd.Kfz.11/1) für 2cm Flak 38 auf le.Zgkw.3t mit Panzerschutz.' Only this one is mounting a M.G. 151/15 auf Schwebelafette Fla-L 151 D/B, or 'Drilling' instead of the 2cm Flak 38. The heavy, full length frontal shield on the 'Drilling' leads us to believe this weapon system was meant to be fitted on a naval vessel rather than an AFV. This particular example does not have any of its three ammo bins mounted so we get a good view of its conical pedestal. Other than a tyre pressure number painted on its fender, no markings are visible on the vehicle.

W.Auerbach

1

A Panzerjäger 38 für 7·62cm Pak 36 (Sd.Kfz.139), its gun defiantly pointing toward the sky as photographed by an Allied soldier somewhere in Germany in 1945. To the right is a 7·5cm Pak 40: the height difference between this and the Panzerjäger is very noticeable here.

L.Archer

Left: The caption to this well-known Signal Corps photo, dated 25 March 1945, states that this Panzer IV/70(V), number '201' was "*abandoned in the face of US First Army troops outside Oberpleis, Germany.*" Fortuitously, it gave us the location where the second, personal photo was taken from the road of vehicle number '202.' This juxtaposition provides a welcome opportunity to compare their markings and camouflage schemes, and for Hans Weber to give us his thoughts: The bottom photo "*reminds me of a picture of a pair of ko'ed Panzerjägers found in the unit history of 3rd Armored. There the tanks are mentioned to be at Oberpleis, no steel wheels at the front, either. This and some basic* knowledge of the disposition of units at this front (Remagen bridgehead) links them to 3. PGD [3.Panzergrenadier-Division]. If indeed taken at the same spot - unfortunately not a sure match - I would make this Stab, 2./Pz.Jg. Abt. 3. For sure, at this time, 3. PGD had an unusually high number of these vehicles (20 as per 15.3.45), although at this date, only 6 were in running condition. 'Toxic' seems to be one of the typical code names used by the US for their units. Haven't found out which, however and QM should be short for Quartermaster. It's thus probably a sign post to lead to the QM of a unknown unit codenamed 'Toxic.'*

1x US Army, 1x L.Archer

This rear three-quarter view lets us make out some of the writing below the gunshield: "*Unsere XXXX*" is painted in white on the plain 'Dunkelgelb' basecoat, the second word too indistinct to recognise. A careful look at the rear superstructure armour reveals that it is missing a number of rivets.

L.Archer

The photographer steps back a few more feet and we get an expanded view of the scene. Buildings in the background and a Jagdpanzer 38 come into view, but the bright sunshine splashing off the glacis of the Jagdpanzer and the gun shield of the Pak 40 affect the exposure. Still, we begin to suspect that we are on the grounds of a Panzerjäger training school.

L.Archer

We have no idea why anyone would go to the trouble to make such an accurate 1:1 scale rendering of a Pz.Kpfw.IV, but here it is. Note that even the ventilator for the driver and the forward lifting hook on the turret have been painted in!

W.Auerbach

Three G.I.s pose against the shattered remains of a Sturmgeschütz III Ausf.G near Aachen at the end of 1944. The side of the hull and superstructure have been cut away, almost surgically, with very straight cuts above the roadwheels for example, but by whom? The trackguards, return rollers and other items from the vehicle are strewn about the ground.

L.Archer

Tank '631' is a Pz.Kpfw.IV Ausf.G with bolted 'Zusatzpanzer' on the driver's front plate and smoke grenade dischargers on the turret front. It was from II./Pz.Rgt.15 of 11.Panzer-Division and was destroyed near Lyon, France. This is the sister vehicle to tank '632' seen on page 19 of *Panzerwrecks 6*, which had a tactical number painted in a solid colour outlined in white, unlike the black outlined number as seen here. It is missing its antenna trough from the side, leaving a dark horizontal line. The 7·5cm Kw.K has been 'truncated' by the crew, leaving it a lot shorter than usual. German tankers were instructed to destroy or demolish their vehicles to prevent a useful item from falling into enemy hands.

L.Archer

Thanks to the work of Jens Mühlig (königstiger332) on Panzer-Archiv.de we know that this Jagdtiger, tactical number '224,' was lost to the s.Pz.Jg.Abt.653 in Iggelheim, Germany on 22 March 1945. In fact he was able to pinpoint the location as outside 37 Sandgasse (the building minus its windows on the left). It was commanded by Unteroffizier Ernst August Hagelstein. Some think it was destroyed by the crew, others that it was hit by artillery. We can say for certain that the gun is out of battery and that daylight can be seen through the bottom of the sponson, indicating that some of the engine deck is missing. It appears that the roof is missing as well.

2x W.Auerbach

In our 'War Booty in Yugoslavia' feature in *Panzerwrecks 2*, we featured photos of several railcars loaded with AFVs of Italian origin, and here we have another train load of interesting vehicles, in particular, two examples of the Sturmgeschütz L6 mit 47/32 770(i) with the early flag of the Yugoslav partisans painted on their sides. This flag was Blue/White (with red star)/Red. Behind the StuGs is a Panzerspähwagen AB41 201 (i). The series of photographs was taken by Albert Kos in Ljubljana on 9 June 1945.

MNZS

Moving down the track, we can see that a Tiefladeanhänger für Panzerkampfwagen (Sd.An.115) stowed with supplies and some Pz.Kpfw.L6/40 733 (i)'s are behind the Panzerspähwagen AB41 201 (i). Behind them is a Panzerspähwagen Panhard 178-P204 (f). A bit of field dentistry goes on in the foreground.

MNZS

A pristine Pz.Kpfw.L6/40 733 (i) provides the backdrop for a group photo. It has a dark red star on its side door and is missing its radio antenna. The second vehicle is missing its main armament and has had its entire gun mantlet pushed back out of its trunnions.

MNZS

Troops climb down between two StuG III Ausf.G's (one without brackets for 'Schürzen') to get a better look at what the others see, while others relax in the warm spring sunshine.

Further down the train are a Pz.Kpfw.M15/42 738 (i), another StuG III and a pair of Pz.Kpfw.38 H 735 (f).

MNZS

This Russian soldier seems transfixed on a 'short-tracked' Sturmgeschütz IV at the Vienna Arsenal in 1945 (note the wide 'Ostketten'). The StuG has had concrete added to the front of the superstructure and carries its drive sprocket on the roof. Also, the muzzle brake is rotated 90° from its normal position. The Arsenal was used as a vehicle maintenance facility by the Germans throughout the war, which explains the number and diversity of armoured vehicles. Apart from a few Pz.Kpfw.I's, most of the armour in the background is of Italian origin.

2x RGAKFD

More wreckage awaiting a repair that will never come. The Panther Ausf.G, tactical number '232,' has had its left track 'short-tracked'. The coarse textured 'Zimmerit' is a feature of Panthers assembled by Daimler-Benz. Two scars are visible on the gun mantlet; one between the coaxial MG aperture and the gun, the other on the far edge of the mantlet. In the background are a Pz.Kpfw.IV Ausf.J, Pz.Kpfw.I, another Panther, and at the edge of the building a Tiger.

RGAKFD

This is the Tiger seen in the background on page 87 of *Panzerwrecks 2*. It belonged to 3./ Pz.Rgt.29 of Panzer-Division Müncheberg. This photograph was taken after the tank had been stripped of useful, and not so useful items, such as the roadwheels, idlers, trackguards and spare tracks. The 'Swastika' painted onto the hull side was probably not the work of the Germans. The sign on the right of the photo reads 'Schleswiger Ufer,' the embankment on the south side of the river Spree.

M.Lippert

A collection of wrecks in the Tiergarten. On the left is a m.ZgKw. 8 ton (Sd.Kfz.7) seen from the rear and a m.Pi.Pz.Wg. (Sd.Kfz.251/7). In the middle is a m.S.P.W. (Sd.Kfz.251), with the unit insignia of 11.SS-Freiw.Pz.Gren-Division 'Nordland' and tactical number '53? on its rear plate. A le.S.P.W. (Sd.Kfz.250) Ausf.B is just visible behind it. On the right is a le.ZgKw. 3 ton (Sd.Kfz.11). Note the lengths of track strewn around and the lack of wheels on the halftracks. **Opposite:** What appears to be a burnt out m.Fu.Pz.Wg. (Sd.Kfz.251/3) radio car dug in in front of the command tower of the Zoobunker.

2x M.Lippert

Modern day technology, and the work of Mario Lippert, means that we can accurately pinpoint the location of this lonely Sturmgeschütz as being on the corner of Invalidenstraße and Brunnenstraße, where Russian and German policemen direct the traffic. The Sturmgeschütz has a 'Rundumfeuer' MG mount by the loader's hatch, steel return rollers and no 'Zimmerit' coating. This photo was taken in June 1945. **RGAKFD**

This Sturmgeschütz III Ausf.F was destroyed on the Voßstraße and photographed on 15 May 1945 by a Russian army photographer. This would appear to be a vehicle assembled before June 1942, when additional armour was welded to the front of the superstructure and hull. Extra armour plate has been added to the sloping surface above and opposite the driver and to the top of the radio panniers. The superstructure roof plate lacks the crew compartment ventilation fan housing so unique to the Ausf.F and F/8.

Ullsteinbild

Signpost text (Cyrillic):
КЮСТРИН
ЦЕНТР
УНТЕР ДЕН ЛИНДЕН
РЕЙХСТАГ
ПОТСДАМ
АЛЬТШТАДТ
СИМЕНСШАДТ

A schwerer Panzerspähwagen (7·5cm Pak 40) (Sd.Kfz.234/4) destroyed at the Nollendorfplatz, where it had taken up position to fire down 'Mackensenstraße' (renamed 'Else-Lasker-Schüler-Straße' today). This vehicle has the hard edged camouflage scheme. With thin armour and only 36 stowed rounds for the Pak 40, this s.Pz.Sp.Wg could not have been expected to put up a protracted fight. Rear mounted driving controls and all wheel steering would have allowed the vehicle to be driven backwards at full speed in an emergency. Note the hinged cover over the radiator for the air cooled diesel engine opens at the front.

W.Auerbach

The original caption reads: *"Nazi tanks still in Berlin, Germany. Pfc. John Shoemaker of Hattiesburg, Miss., looks over some wrecked German army vehicles still to be seen in the Tiergarten section of Berlin. Machines apparently were moved here by the Germans to be burned when defeat was but a matter of hours."* The machines in question are s.Pz.Sp.Wg. (7·5cm) (Sd.Kfz.234/4) and belonged to Pz.Aufkl.Kp. Müncheberg of Panzer-Division Müncheberg or St./Pz.Aufkl.Abt.118 of 18.Panzergrenadier-Division.

L.Archer/W.Auerbach

A ground fog receded just enough to let a photographer record a panoramic view of a collection of Sturmgeschütz III Ausf.G's and heavy eight-wheeled armoured cars on the outskirts of Berlin, possibly Brandenburg. For the most part, the StuG's had coaxial MG's in their mantlets and remote controlled MG's on their roofs. The armoured cars were either schwerer Panzerspähwagen (Sd.Kfz.231) (8 Rad) or the Fu 12 equipped s.Pz.Sp.Wg. (Fu) (Sd.Kfz.232) (8 Rad) and had cast visors and 30mm frontal armour. **RGAKFD**

The cameraman has panned to the right. The Sturmgeschütz III Ausf.G on the left of has two clean penetrations in its nose armour, the vehicle in the middle is missing its roadwheels and engine compartment cover, while the StuG on the right has suffered some sort of internal fire as the front torsion bars have sagged, lowering the drive sprocket almost to the ground.

RGAKFD

27

Russian SU-76's trundle past a dug in Pz.Kpfw.IV on Frankfurter Allee that had been operated by Pz.Kp. (bo) Berlin. This unit was raised for the defence of Berlin on 22 February 1945 and was equipped with 12 immobile Pz.Kpfw.IV and 10 immobile Panthers, each crewed with a commander, gunner and loader. A clear and distinct camouflage pattern is visible on the rear plate of the turret.

BPK

German workers use brute force to remove parts from this dug in Pz.Kpfw.IV which is destined for the smelting pot. An explosion has left the turret without a commander's cupola and buckled the roof armour. The lack of vision and pistol ports on the turret side doors indicate that this is an Ausf.J version, the pistol ports in the rear turret wall were due to be deleted by May 1944, but many Ausf.J were completed with them. The sprayed camouflage pattern can be clearly seen.

Ullsteinbild

A Russian officer proudly stands by another of Pz.Kp. (bo) Berlin's dug in tanks, this one a Panther on the corner of Möllendorffstraße and Frankfurter Allee. A Russian anti-tank shell has made short work of the Panther's 100mm thick gun mantlet, punching a hole clean through it. The camouflage pattern on the 7·5cm gun barrel is reminiscent of that used on British Sherman Fireflies with a dark wavy pattern on the top of the barrel and a lighter shade underneath.

RGAKFD

The same Panther, shown here with a constant stream of Russian soldiers passing by. The rising smoke is perhaps an indication that this photo was taken not long after Berlin fell. The shell responsible for holing the Panther's mantlet has hit the back of the turret, cracking it and blowing off the commander's cupola and rear hatch. **RGAKFD**

Two children pose with a Panzer IV/70(A) in a 'Standard' filling station in the Alsace. A photo of the front end of this vehicle was published on page 85 of *Panzerwrecks 1*, but the original was poor quality. Although not much better, we can see that it is in fact a Befehlswagen as it has the armoured pot for the extra antenna base on the back of the fighting compartment. The loader's hatch is fitted with a 'Vorsatz-P' mounting for an MP44. Spare roadwheels; one resilient steel and one rubber tyred were carried on the engine deck. **Inset**: The complete scene.

L.Archer

A G.I. leans against a trackless Panzer IV/70(A). Although the Panzer has been stripped of many things, it retains some of the spare tracks fitted to the driver's front plate, such as those seen in *Panzerwrecks 1*. The gun travel lock has been disassembled and the tracks have gone. A careful look at the MG port beside the gun shows an MG42 in place.

W.Auerbach

Štítina railway station in the summer of 1945: among the wrecks collected is this Panzer IV/70(V), which probably belonged to Pz.Abt.7 of 10.Pz.Gren-Division. An unusual feature of this vehicle is the placement of spare track links on the sides of the superstructure. It also has three return rollers and has an AP scoop on the front of the mantlet. A m.S.P.W. (7·5cm Kanone) (Sd.Kfz.251/9) is among the wrecked T34s is in the background of page 35. **2x VHU**

This 4·7cm Pak (t) (Sfl.) auf Fgst.Pz.Kpfw.35 R 731 (f), tactical number '111,' was found between Ypres and Bailieul by a Canadian officer, who reported that there were "*minor mechanical defects and it had been abandoned*". That, and the fact it was in a ditch. By the summer of 1944, most of these vehicles were serving piecemeal in reserve units in the West.

2x LAC

The breech mechanism of the 4·7cm Pak(t) shows that it was built in 1941 by Škodawerke in Plzeň (Pilsen), 'bxb' being their manufacturer's code. This somewhat rare view into the fighting compartment shows how the top of the hull was cut to convert it into a Panzerjäger, with part of the old turret ring visible next to the gun. The gunner's position was to the left of the gun. To his left, on the wall of the superstructure, is what looks like an empty radio rack.

LAC

A burnt out Bergepanther and Panther Ausf.A share a common rail line to oblivion. Both have DEMAG's distinctive horizontal ridge 'Zimmerit' pattern, although fire has burnt away most of it. The Bergepanther has the base mount for the 2cm Kw.K.38. No information is available as to when or where this photo was taken, or by whom, although it was likely that the vehicles were on their way back to be repaired and refitted.

W.Auerbach

A vehicle collection dump is an odd place to take a date. Odder still is the Pz.Kpfw.IV chassis mounting an 8.8cm Flak 37 that they climbed onto, and oddest of all is the fact there were at least two such vehicles here at Bory airfield, just outside Plzeň (Pilsen), Czechoslovakia.

1x AMC, 1x D.Brown

The Fahrgestell Nr. '80431' on this Pz.Kpfw.IV chassis makes it an Ausf.C. Flush brake access hatches with armoured cowls, 40cm wide track and a 'Bosch' headlamp indicate that someone was keeping this vehicle upgraded. This is a different vehicle to the one on the opposite page as it has a gun crutch, tracks, forged rather than cast roadwheel caps and steel return rollers. The 'S' in a rhomboid with an arrow on top indicates its use in a heavy anti-tank unit. The Jagdpanzer 38 on the right of the photo sports a Škoda camouflage pattern.

D.Brown

Two views of Bory Airfield looking like an alternate Aberdeen Proving Ground chock full of interesting AFVs and rarities as far as the eye can see, including a Panzer-Schulfahrzeuge (driver training vehicle), m.S.P.W. Ausf.C (Sd.Kfz.251), schwerer Panzerspähwagen (5cm) (Sd.Kfz.234/2), several Jagdpanzer 38's, a pair of 'Hummels,' schwerer Panzerspähwagen (7.5cm) (Sd.Kfz.234/3), a kleiner Panzerbefehlswagen (Sd.Kfz.265) with truncated suspension, and our old favourite.

1x E.Bealko, 1x L.Archer

A close-up of the schwerer Panzerspähwagen (7·5cm) (Sd.Kfz.234/3) from the previous page showing its outlined tactical number '053' and opened hull escape hatch catching the light. This vehicle belonged to Pz.A.A.20 of 20.Panzer-Division, who surrendered to the US 16th Armored Division on 9 May 1945. This was covered in *Panzerwrecks 4*, in fact this vehicle is probably the one that we show on page 18. The Jagdpanzer 38 was probably moved from the remnants of the nearby Škoda factory. **L.Archer**

A close-up of the photo at the bottom of page 42. In the foreground we have a 1.Serie/ kl.Pz.Bef.Wg. (Sd.Kfz.265), identifiable by its lack of commander's cupola. Unusually, this diminutive vehicle has been 'short-tracked' on both sides, since no idlers are fitted. Behind this is the 8·8cm Flak/Pz.Kpfw.IV oddball, and to the right of that is a Jagdpanzer 38 Befehlswagen, note the large armoured 'cowl' on the left side of the fighting compartment for the extra radio antenna. **Opposite**: Close-ups from the top of page 42. In the top photo, behind the m.S.P.W. (Sd.Kfz.251) - which is probably from SS-Pz.Gren.Rgt.4 'Der Führer' - is the back end of a Bergepanzer 38. **1x L.Archer, 3x E.Bealko**

44

This superb example of a schwerer Panzerspähwagen (5cm) (Sd.Kfz.234/2), tactical number '022', can be seen on the previous page, sandwiched between the m.S.P.W. and 8·8cm Flak/Pz.Kpfw.IV oddball. Like the Sd.Kfz.234/3 seen earlier on, it belonged to Pz.A.A.20, 20.Panzer-Division. The 'Hummel' in the background has a white tank painted on the front of the superstructure.

L.Archer

G.I.'s climb on the 'Hummels'. On the left of the top photo is a tempting glimpse of a Sd.Kfz.234/1 turret and top of a Bergepanzer 38, while in the lower photo a G.I. stands on another Sd.Kfz.234/1. Smaller vehicles, such as the kleines Kettenkrad and Pz.Kpfw.I in the photo at right, fill in the spaces between the larger vehicles. **3x AMC**

These two AMR-35's armed with 7·5mm Hotchkiss MG were probably from 'Pz.Kp. Prag'. Behind, the 'Marder 38T' apparently lacks part of the gun shield and behind this are various Zugkraftwagen and Selbstfahrlafette, both armoured and unarmoured. The Jagdpanzer 38 on the left has a 4 hole idler. **Inset**: A G.I. commands an AMR-35. **Opposite**: A mortar carrier based on an AMR-35.

1x L.Archer, 1x D.Brown, 4x US Army

49

A veteran named Karl W. Speckman photographed these two Panther turrets in Braunschweig, Germany, in 1945. The turret on the left still has the Kursk era smoke grenade dischargers fitted and appears to have the Ausf.D type sides to the mantlet. It sits on a higher mounting. The other turret is that of an Ausf.A with cast cupola and vane sight. Its lower, mobile platform (with wheels from a Pz.Kpfw.III or StuG III) leads us to believe that these turrets could have been used for gunnery practice. Both turrets have pistol ports in their sides with their plugs hanging down on chains.

D.Brown

A m.S.P.W. Ausf.C, tactical number '123,' with a field mounted M.G. 151 auf Schwebelafette Fla-L 151 D/B or 'Drilling.' This example is pointing in the 11 o'clock position and has a low, rectangular shield fitted to the front only. The overturned object on the left of the picture is a 15cm sIG33. This very poor quality image was taken by a Russian photographer in East Prussia in 1945.

TsAMO

Torgau, April 1945. Russian troops roll up to meet the Americans in a mittlerer Schützenpanzerwagen (Drilling) (Sd.Kfz.251/21) Ausf.D with lower pedestal. The m.S.P.W. has the rear hinged engine hatch and flat visors, and would have made quite an entrance as the exhaust is missing its muffler. The Russians have painted over the original stencils, markings, numbers, etc. **Opposite:** The travel lock on the bottom of the shield is readily apparent in this photo. This vehicle mounted the M.G.151/20 guns without flash hiders.

2x NARA

Beat up, burnt out, and picked over, this mittlerer Schützenpanzer (7·5cm Pak) (Sd. Kfz.251/22) is nevertheless interesting. The side hinged radiator cover, gun travel lock and missing blanking plate for the visor on the co-driver's side all offer details to study. The track has broken, probably while the vehicle was reversing judging by the 'snake' of track by the drive sprocket. The shiny track pads indicate that it was fitted with 'Stahlkappen,' (steel caps), so would have been rather noisy on hard surfaces and limited to a speed of 30km/h on the road. The small clips along the roof lead us to believe that this vehicle was converted from a m.S.P.W. (7·5cm Kanone) (Sd.Kfz.251/9) at the factory. **AMC**

Offered for comparison is this unburnt m.S.P.W. (7·5cm Pak) (Sd.Kfz.251/22). The smooth waves and spots of camouflage paint blend the vehicle in nicely to its wooded environment. In fact, a careful study of this camouflage paint-job with that of the vehicle on the previous page shows them to be very similar with light patches showing in the same areas on both, a result of a factory applied camouflage scheme. The outer roadwheels and front wheels are missing, a common sight on many m.S.P.W. wrecks. Unfortunately, we can't make out the markings on the nose armour.

TTM

A British soldier demonstrates how this Panther hull would be drawn from station to station on a wheeled trolley through the tank assembly plant of the MNH (Maschinenfabrik Niedersachsen Hanover) factory soon after it was overrun. A large label reads *"Achtung. Ladung zu breit auf beiden seite"* (*"Attention: Load overhangs on both sides"*), but it is unknown if this was for rail transport to the factory of for movement within the factory. It is interesting that, even at an early stage in assembly, before the suspension has been fitted, smaller, more delicate items have been added to the hull.

TTM

56

Panther hulls are stacked up three high in the turret machining bay where turret rings were installed. Gantry cranes ran the length of the bays to aid in assembly. **Page 58**: A Jagdpanther hull being machined ready to receive the final drive housing early in the process. The Panther and Jagdpanther had the same frontal armour thicknesses and angles: glacis 80mm at 55° and lower front plate 50mm at 55°.

2x TTM

MNH assembled both the Panther Ausf.G and Jagdpanther Ausf.G2. The company was scheduled to assemble 890 Panther Ausf.G between July 1944 and May 1945, but only 806 were produced before the factory was overrun in April of 1945. At first, Jagdpanther assembly at MNH was seen as a temporary stop gap measure to quickly produce 80 Jagdpanthers between November 1944 and January 1945 after MIAG was bombed, but the deteriorating war situation led to MNH planning to continue production at 20 units per month from February onward in addition to its normal Panther production. MNH eventually produced 112 Jagdpanthers in all, 43 from February to April. **TTM**

Looking down into the vast galleries where vehicles were fitted with their automotive components. After driving and acceptance tests were completed, the chassis would go to an adjacent building to receive their turrets and main armament. **Opposite**: Jagdpanther assembly predominates this scene of the shop floor as Maybach HL 230 P30 power plants are installed. At this point the double visors for the driver have been dropped in favour of a single visor. New components, such as transmissions with auxiliary drives for charcoal bed poison gas defence, were still being introduced as late as January 1945 and beyond.

2x TTM

The Jagdpanthers seen on the left of the previous page. Motion picture cameramen from the USAAF were dispatched to MNH to document damage to the factory, and the difference in attitude between the British, who were more concerned about the layout and operation of the plant, and the Army Air Force personnel, who were more concerned with damage to the plant, is clearly evident, with scene after scene of collapsed trusswork and missing roofs being filmed upward from floor level. With unusual candor, the Americans in their Strategic Bombing Surveys admitted to rather lacklustre results in their campaign against German tank production, stating that *"...damage from area raids was more serious than that caused by plant raids."*

NARA

The Jagdpanthers seen on page 62 but from the other end. Here they wait in line to receive their road wheels and new, larger idlers. The British Army of the Rhine elected to complete assembly of a number of these vehicles, and within nine months was able to complete nine Panthers and twelve Jagdpanthers for evaluation trials, of which both a Panther and Jagdpanther survive at Bovington Tank Museum. The full story can be found in David Fletcher's article, 'British Panthers', which appeared in issue 62 of 'Wheels & Tracks' magazine. Note how the swing arms, idler and lower hull have been painted in a darker, presumably the finished, colour as they will be inaccessible once the wheels and tracks have been fitted.

NARA

The mix of incendiary bombs and HE was designed to blow off the roofs of the factories and let the incendiaries do their work on the more sensitive wiring and equipment beneath. Here a Jagdpanther's hull appears scorched and blackened amid the building rubble, indicating that the USAAF's one-two punch had reached at least one of its intended targets.

NARA

A rear view of a Jagdpanther shows the 'Flammvernichter' mufflers installed. The Automotive Wing of the Fighting Vehicle Proving Establishment tested these vehicles in 1948, and, even with the utmost attention given to engine maintenance, testers found that the carburettor flooded and "*long jets of flame*" spewed from "*white hot exhaust pipes*" presaging engine fires.

NARA

In a scene more reminiscent of a twisted rail yard or refinery, this portion of the MNH factory reveals extensive damage to its roof and overhead cranes but little damage to its floors, which one would think would be covered in debris. MNH was still completing turrets with a mix of curved and 'chin' mantlets at the end of the war, and it looks as though some G.I.'s rotated the turrets to amuse themselves. Although the MG rings on the cupolas had been dispensed with, the turrets still lacked the five rings to hold camouflage in place. None of these turrets appears to have been fitted with its turret basket.

2x NARA

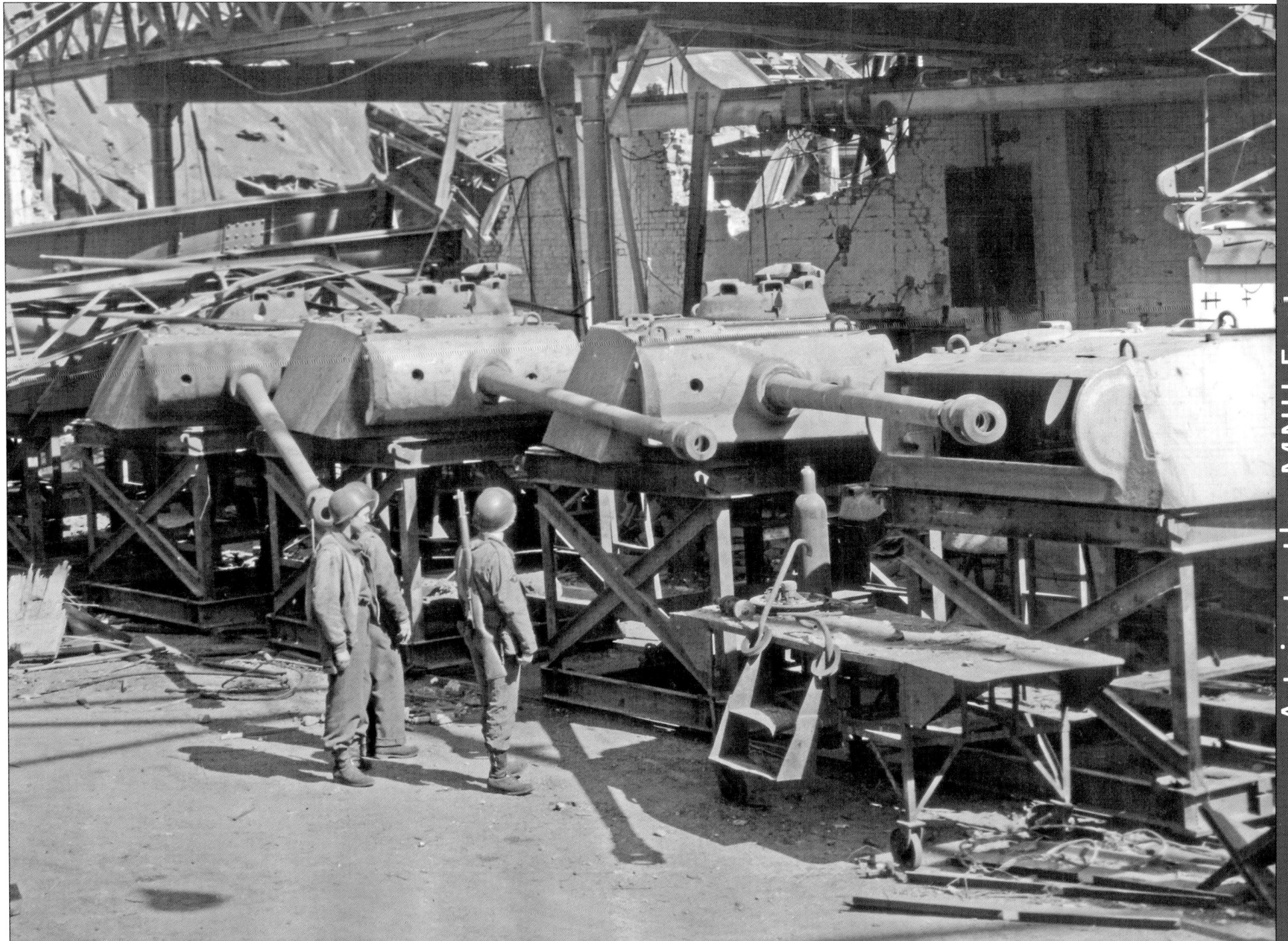

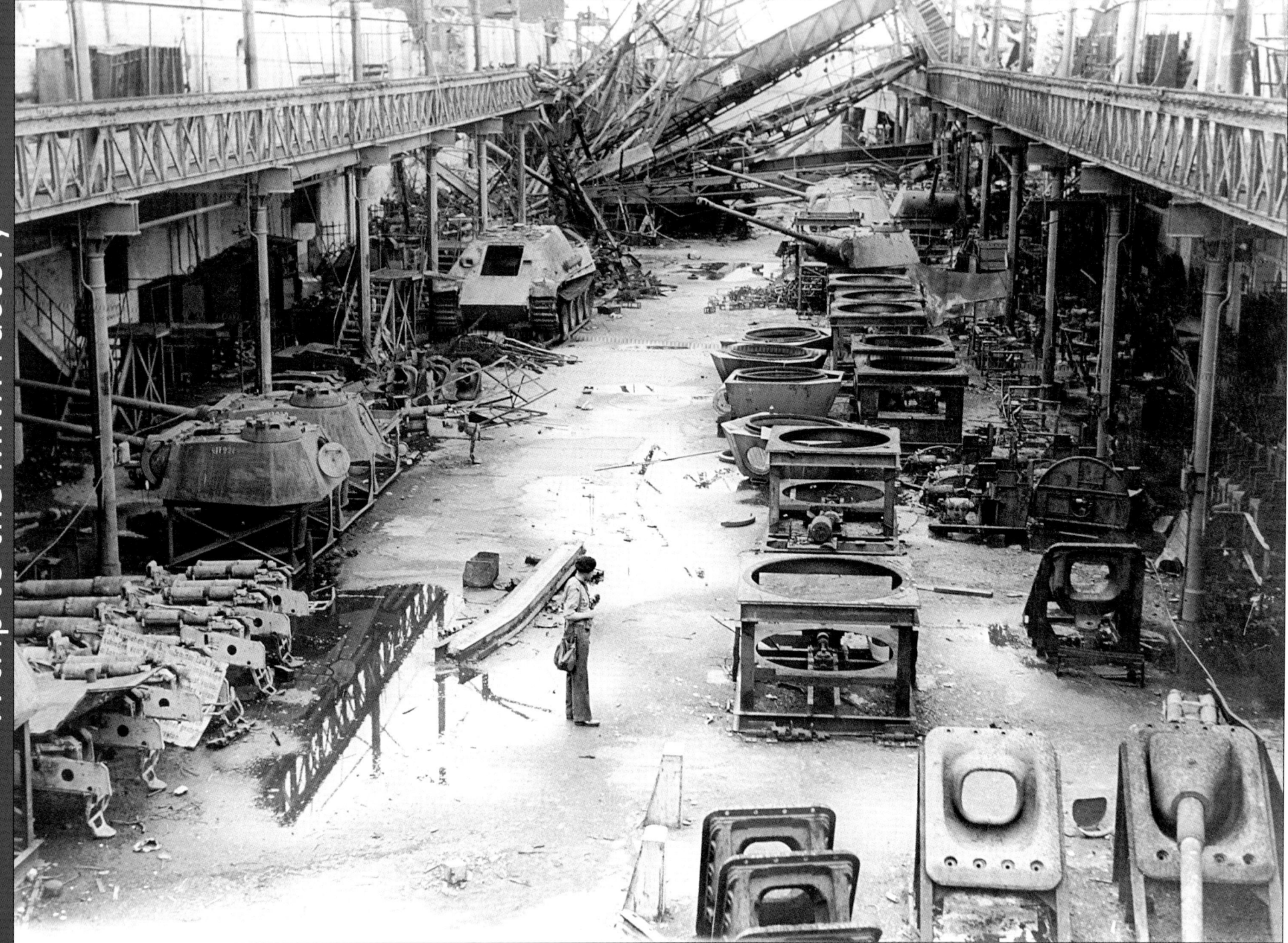

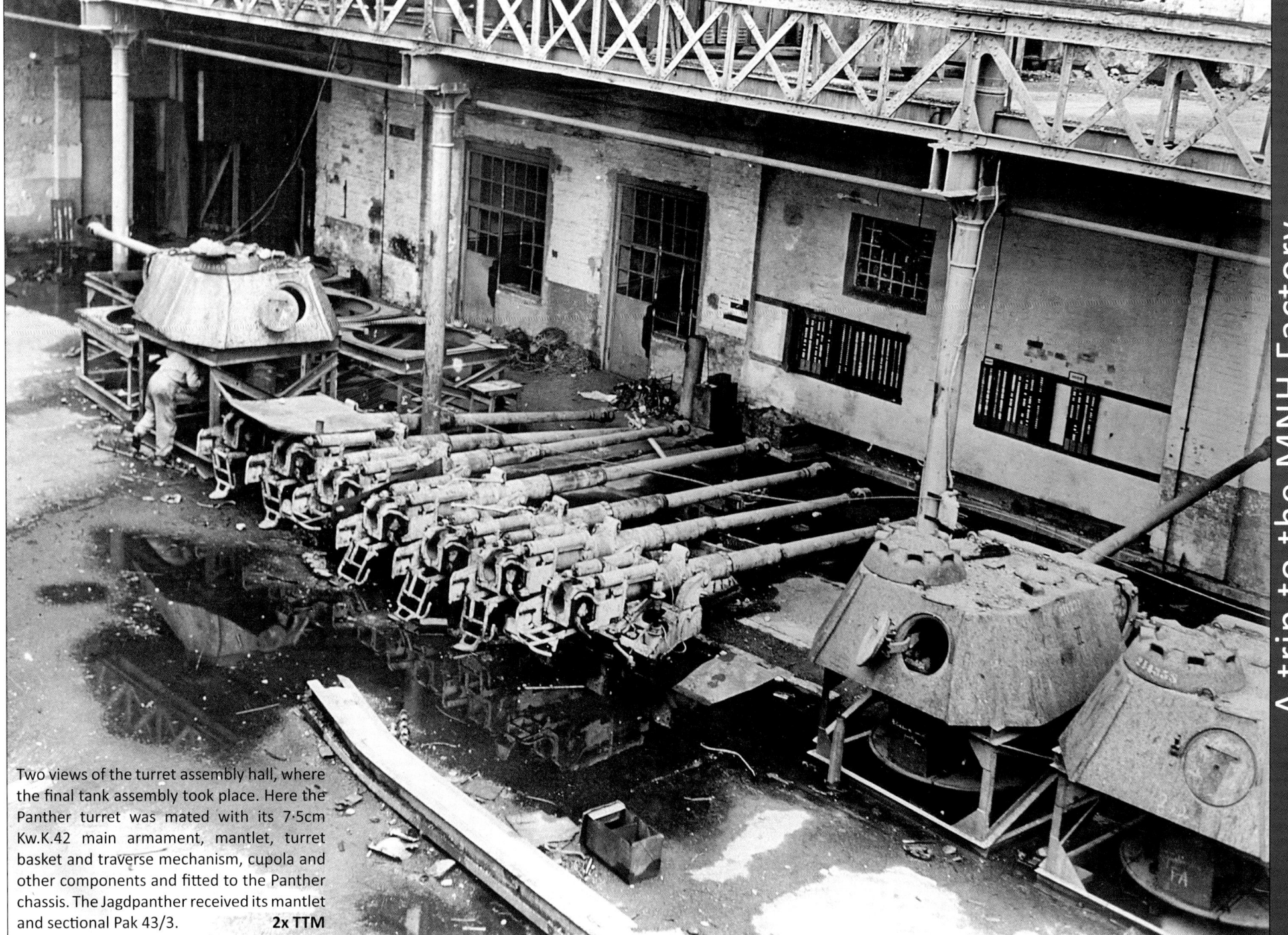

Two views of the turret assembly hall, where the final tank assembly took place. Here the Panther turret was mated with its 7·5cm Kw.K.42 main armament, mantlet, turret basket and traverse mechanism, cupola and other components and fitted to the Panther chassis. The Jagdpanther received its mantlet and sectional Pak 43/3. **2x TTM**

A young boy, perhaps performing for the cameraman, sights down the barrel of an 8·8cm Pak 43/3 as if it were no more than a toy to be played with. He may also have tried his hand at drawing the 'Kilroy' cartoon head on the Panther turret next to him, but it, like everything else at the plant, remains unfinished. **NARA**

Two German civilians in the process of evacuating the shell torn town of Oberkirchen, Germany, stop to look at a Pz.Kpfw.IV Ausf.J on 5 April 1945. The Panzer had been knocked out by a tank destroyer unit of the US 7th Armored Division. Note the small plates for holding 'Losterkennungstafeln' (poison gas detection cards) hanging over the side of the turret 'Schürzen' and apparent small calibre penetration of the upper rear plate. **US Army**

The tank seen on the previous page (on the right) with a Pz.Bef.Wg.IV. The identifiers for it being a Pz.Bef.Wg rather than a standard tank are the antenna fitted to the rear of the engine deck and the antenna base on the turret roof, just next to the turret ventilator. Both tanks belonged to Kampfgruppe Hudel, which was the reinforced I./Pz.Rgt.130, and during March 1945, was subordinated to the 11.Panzer-Division. This unit fought in Oberkirchen on 3 and 4 April 1945 against US forces. The two tanks have features that we would expect to see on final production Pz.Kpfw.IV such as: extended hull side tow points, simplified hull lifting loops, wire mesh 'Schürzen' with mesh covers over the top, deleted gunner's vision port, swivelling commander's hatch, and the holy grail; handles on the brake access hatches instead of cast cowlings.

2x AMC

What at first looks like a fairly standard Pz.Kpfw.IV is in fact something quite rare; a Pz.Beob. Wg.IV. We showed two vehicles of this type in *Panzerwrecks 2*, but they were in bad shape. This example looks to be in running condition and this photo is the first, as far as we know, that shows the configuration of the turret roof. The most obvious difference to a standard Pz.Kpfw.IV is the use of a Sturmgeschütz cupola with its 7 periscopes and the ability to use a SF14Z scissors periscope while buttoned up. A T.S.R.1 observation periscope was fitted in a mount to the left of the cupola, but it is obscured here by a box like item. An extra antenna base has been fitted on a plate where the 'Nahverteidigungswaffe' would normally be, next to the turret ventilator, which itself is a later type with thicker armour. Mesh covers have been fitted on top of the hull 'Schürzen', while the long slim box in the left of the photo held spare antennas.

2x L.Archer

A Polish tanker stands in the roofless wreck of a Sturmgeschütz III Ausf.G near Moerdijk, Netherlands in November 1944. These photographs clearly show the factory applied camouflage paint scheme and the light colour of the opened brake access hatches. The vehicle is from the post-September production run as it lacks 'Zimmerit' and has the aperture in the mantlet for a coaxial MG. Quite where the gun barrel has gone is a bit of a mystery, as it is not lying on the ground as we might expect. One of the original captions states that this is *"a Polish Sherman tank battling through German defences."*

3x PISM

Opposite: A turretless Pz.Kpfw.IV Ausf.B or C chassis uparmoured with 30mm 'Zusatzpanzerung' on the hull front and bolt-on 30mm armour on the superstructure front. The jigsaw puzzle type cut outs in the bolt on armour are to accommodate the pistol port next to the radio operator's visor and the periscopic vision device for the driver. The vehicle was either in use as a munitions carrier or driver training vehicle since it was not de-turreted by Allied gunfire. The significance of the letter 'D' on a white circle is unknown.

L.Archer

An odd Panther, Ausf.D or A, sits sandwiched between another Panther and a T34. The middle Panther is probably one of the early Versuchs vehicles being used as a steel wheel test bed. This photo is that it is attributed to an 'Alan Pavenza,' and was taken *"in West Europe, 1944 or '45. Probably Germany, 1945"* and was part of a collection of photos belonging to James V. Crow.

D.Brown

Why waste valuable fuel for training? These unusual hybrids were photographed by a G.I. named Karl W. Speckman in Braunschweig, Germany in 1945. They are 'Panzerattrappen' based upon the chassis of 'Panzer-Schulfahrzeuge' (training vehicles) powered by 'Holzvergas' generators and fitted with mock Pz.Kpfw.III turrets and superstructures. The little vehicles have typical German attention to detail and include radio antennas, authentic looking cupolas and elevating mock weapons. Parts of the vehicles are fabricated from wood and sheet metal, as can be seen on the hinged roof panels and rather thick turret hatches on the vehicle in the foreground and turret cut outs on the vehicle in the background. The rear vehicle has had the side of its turret ripped away revealing its wooden construction. The middle vehicle lacks its superstructure and turret, only the supporting metalwork remains. Panther hulls lurk in the background and behind the vehicle in the foreground. **Inset**: Another example, possibly at a different location with a different design of hatches on the turret sides. **1x D.Brown, 1x L.Archer**

The same two G.I.s pose in a Pz.Kpfw.I Ausf.A. Its Fahrgestell Nr. '10091' makes this a Henschel assembled vehicle from the 2.Serie. Behind it are a pair of pre-July 1943 vintage Panther Ausf.D hulls. The foremost Panther has 16 bolt road wheels and a fitting for a vertically mounted 450mm 'C'-clamp on the hull. This vehicle was possibly one of the first Panthers manufactured as the area under the 'C'-clamp is in the original RAL 7021 'Dunkelgrau' colour; it received a RAL 7028 'Dunkelgelb' overspray later. From the amount of rust on the tracks, it appears that none of these vehicles has moved in quite some time. **Inset**: The non-standard tool box on hull side of this Ausf.D is typical of those on Panthers issued to Pz.Abt.51 for the Kursk offensive. A large number '2' on its glacis indicating that it was probably used as a 'Panzer-Schulfahrzeuge.' **2x D.Brown**

Freaks and Antiques

An airbrushed version of this photo appeared in *Illustrated Record of German Army Equipment* as Fig.34, identified as being 'Hull of Semi Tracked Tractor Model HK 605.' Further details come from BAOR Technical Intelligence Report No. 49 dated 16 November 1945 entitled *Developments in German Semi-Tracked Vehicles*: "The DEMAG works at Wetter/Ruhr were visited on 2 Oct, 12 Oct and 1 Nov 45, and Herr Jerzembeck, designer, was interviewed. Incomplete specimens of two new models of light semi-track, the HK 605 and HKp 606 were inspected and a number of drawings secured." In the background are several D7p chassis for the Sd.Kfz.250 lacking their outer roadwheels. **TTM**

82

"The armour somewhat resembled that of the Sd.Kfz.251, but was re-arranged. The engine compartment was protected by 30mm armour in the front, and was continuous and watertight underneath. Cooling air enters through louvres at the tip rear end of the bonnet and is discharged via two channels at the sides of the engine compartment through two openings at either side, approximately level with the louvres, there being a baffle plate across the compartment. This ensures a good fording depth. The bonnet armour was continued outwards at either side and in front to provide cover for the front wheels, (eliminating sheet metal mudguards) and protect the headlights, which are mounted behind it, and shine through slits." The HK 605/HKp 606 had a hull construction like the Sd.Kfz.250 rather than the frame construction of a Sd.Kfz.251.

"The engine was a Maybach HL 50. The gearbox was to have been an Olvar pre-selective hydraulically operated type, supplied by Adler, Frankfurt, but this had not been received... There were [five] bogie wheels per side. They were of the disc type with double rubber tyres, and were not interleaved, but staggered, with some overlap ('Staffelaufwerke'). All the bogie wheels were identical, being merely reversed on the radius arm spindles to change from being inner to outer wheels, or vice versa... The steering wheel is not inverted." The HK 605 "has the same general features as the HKp 606 but the armour extends only as far back as the driver's seat, the rear of the vehicle being open. The vehicle is intended for the transport of personnel and as a tractor, not as an AFV."

TTM

Joe Mc Kenna stands with a line up of obsolete vehicles that are still interesting. From left to right: A Pz.Kpfw.I with the superstructure and turret on a Pz.Kpfw.II Ausf.a2 dropped on top, a tactical number of 'I07' on the turret and Panzer rhomboid 1/L (Lehr) on the front superstructure. The next vehicle appears to be a turretless Pz.Kpfw.I with an engine deck dropped on it and missing its towing lugs. The tactical number on the side is 'V4.' Filling out the row are three gepanzerter Munitionsschlepper (Sd.Kfz.111) sporting Balkenkreuze. **Inset**: Two gp.Mun. Schlepper (Sd.Kfz.111) auf fgst Pz.Kpfw.I Ausf.A at a captured weapons collection point southwest of Stalingrad, January 1943, both sporting a two-tone camouflage scheme. **1x L.Archer, 1x NARA**

A line up of the ugly, obsolete and trackless vehicles at a 'Fahrschule' (driving school) as photographed by Joe Mc Kenna. From left to right: a Pz.Kpfw.38(t) chassis with 'Holzvergaser,' two Pz.Kpfw.II chassis with 'Holzvergaser,' one with high wood superstructure sides with vision ports cut out, vicious looking 'Captain Hook' tow hooks and what we can only describe as a 'belly button.' Next to this is a Panzer-Schulfahrzeuge with 'Holzvergaser.' The last vehicle, which has its tracks, is not readily identifiable. The tall cylindrical towers at the rear of the vehicles are gasifier units. They contained the hoppers to hold the wood or charcoal at the top and the combustion chamber to burn them at the bottom, the idea being to make combustible gas from wood or coal. The 'pipes' are water filled precipitating tanks used to remove tars and fine ash from the gas before it went to the engine manifold in order to prevent clogging. Crews had to be careful when opening the lid of the gasifier to 'refuel' that they weren't overcome by carbon monoxide, a by-product of this process.

L.Archer

A G.I. poses on a Sturmgeschütz III Ausf.G with four hooks along the bow, presumably for spare track, as the superstructure is covered with them. The interesting vehicle is to its left, a diminutive 'Panzer-Schulfahrgestell' with a mini 'Holzvergaser' that looks more like an outboard motor.

L.Archer

A Pz.Kpfw.IV Ausf.C chassis, with 30mm 'Zusatzpanzerung' backfitted, is seen here mounting an Ausf.F turret with split commander's hatch and 7·5cm Kw.K.40 gun. The spare track on its hull is the Kgs 61/400/120 track that would not fit on the Ausf.C suspension components designed for the earlier 6110/380/120 track. A Pz.Kpfw.III Ausf.G with 'Vorpanzer' on its turret front is in the background (with its turret turned) and a Renault UE tractor is in the foreground. The UE tractor has four cylinders mounted in the rear, possibly for 'Betriebgas,' but what was the large bracket at the rear for? **USAHEC**

Lee's keen eyes picked out a number scrawled on the right track guard, '60355.' It turns out it's the Fahrgestell Nr. of the 15th Panzerbefehlswagen III Ausf D1 out of thirty produced with fixed turret, dummy gun, one MG34 in the mantlet, thicker armour, additional pistol ports and pivotable antenna mounts. The large frame antenna is missing from the engine deck. On page 89 our G.I. is in the commander's cupola. The vehicle has been repainted in RAL 7028 'Dunkelgelb,' received a black 'Balkenkreuz' on the hull side and loading stencil on the turret.

2x W.Auerbach

A Jagdtiger, probably from s.Pz.Jg.Abt.653, that has been destroyed by the crew by placing demolition charges inside the crew compartment and in the gun, blowing the roof off and cutting the barrel. The vehicle had been cloaked in what looks like a camouflage net, much of which remains. It is thought that the location is Unterbrunn, north of Starnberg, Germany.

L.Archer

How many G.I.s can you get on a Jagdtiger? At least 11 so it appears. The Jagdtiger in question is one of 9 fitted with the Porsche suspension. Two of the suspension units have come off; one lies next to the snake of track, the other in the foreground. Like most Jagdtigers with this suspension system, it has 18 toothed drive sprockets. It is thought that this was a s.Pz.Jg.Akt.653 vehicle which was eventually bulldozed from the road, turning it upside down in the process. **W.Auerbach**

For a number of years it has been assumed that this Tiger had been knocked out in Genval, Belgium. Not so. The key to solving the puzzle was the discovery of the inset photo on the opposite page, which gave the location as Berlebeck, Germany. Hans Weber's and Matthias Radu's sharp eyes picked up on the 'PESAG' Detmold - Berlebeck tram track running down the side of the road. Given the location, this Tiger would have belonged to Pz.Gruppe Paderborn and would have been destroyed in April 1945. A shot into the lower nose armour and driver's front plate (to the side of the radio operator) can be seen. The nearest drive sprocket is dislocated.

L.Archer

The Tiger has some odd and unexplained 'additions' to its turret. First, a rectangular aperture has been cut into the turret roof right over the gunner's head. But what is its purpose? Likewise the circular mark (that bears more than a passing resemblance to a weld seam) around it? And what were the two brackets for on the turret roof, mounted seemingly perfectly above the gun? A training aid? The number '5' appears as a faint outline next to the gunner's vision port. **Inset**: A civilian collects flowers, or tank parts, as photographed by Charles Selby in May 1945.

1x L.Archer, 1x USAHEC

All but one of the photos in this series were taken by a British soldier, who had the forethought to take one or two details shots of the dead Tiger. Here we can see how the 'Zimmerit' coating looks and the thickness of the armour plates. One of the roadwheels is sitting at an odd angle, possibly through damage to the torsion bar. The pistol port on the turret rear is missing its armoured plug. What is the circular marking on the turret bin? Perhaps a unit insignia?

L.Archer

The rear of the Tiger. Most of the fittings are missing with the exception of the towing clevis on the rear plate. The truncated gun was probably the work of the crew who like all Panzertruppen, were trained to destroy their vehicle to deny its use to the enemy. We assume that a charge would have been put in the gun barrel; blowing it up and a charge set inside the tank, which might explain why some of the hatches are missing. The heavy rear turret escape hatch is open and missing its locking mechanism. **L.Archer**

One of the earliest Flakpanzer designs that later became the 'Wirbelwind' was developed by Hauptscharführer Karl Wilhelm Krause of the Pz.Fla-Zug of St./SS-Pz.Rgt.12, and here we see it knocked out in Orbec, France, in the summer of 1944. It was photographed by the Canadians and, in spite of being burnt out, was later covered in a tech intelligence report from where the small photos originate. Here, the missing tow shackle is on the glacis under the ball mounted MG, and the hatch cover for the final drive is between the driver and radio operator's hatches.

1x LAC, 3x NARA